# *Walking*
# *Journal*

©2015 by Wandering Walks of Wonder Publishing

Printed in the United States of America

All rights reserved. No part of this work covered by the copyrights hereon may be reproduced or used in any form or by any means – graphic, electronic or mechanical – without the prior written permission of the publishers, except for reviewers who may quote brief passages. Any request for photocopying, recording, taping or storage on information retrieval systems of any part of this work shall be directed in writing to the publisher.

The Publisher: Wandering Walks of Wonder Publishing

Kansas City, MO 64118

USA


Website: www.wanderingwalksofwonder.com


ISBN-13: 978-1514845042

ISBN-10: 1514845040

## This Journal Belongs to:

_____

To All those Who Walk, Wander, Wonder, and Dream

Inside this journal you will find areas to record your walks, space for personal reflection, and inspiration to greet you with each new walk.

Even though walking is a sport that will never garner the support of its own team of cheerleaders, walking is well worth it and allows everyone to pursue various fitness goals.

For those beginning a walking program, there are a few basics to practice that will make the experience an enjoyable one – the most important being: start slowly. One of the greatest obstacles to any fitness program is over enthusiasm - where the first effort performed at a high level of intensity is so severe that the pain experienced discourages you from trying again.

Secondly, a flat terrain is probably the best place to start, since it is easy to navigate and more predictable. Check out local parks or even a school's running track (often these are rubber coated) for great places to walk.

Whether you walk on a local trail, meander through a city park, or hike in the woods, walking is a great way to get in shape, reduce stress, and even to solve problems.

Use the spaces in this journal to record your walks and jot down notes on how you feel, problems you solved while walking, or just simply the sights and sounds you saw along the way. Then, when you need the motivation to go out and walk, look at your reflections to find the joy in walking.

# *Walking Tips*

- Shoes: Comfortable footwear is a must, and should address the specifics of your feet including such issues as high arches, flat feet, past injuries, and the joints of your ankles.

- Heart Rate: It's always a good idea to check your heart rate as you walk. There are many devices that can be worn on the wrist like a watch to monitor your heart rate.

- Buy a pedometer: Pedometers are devices that measure the distance you have walked, are usually very discreet in appearance, and great for totaling daily, weekly, and monthly goals.

- Walk with a friend: Conversation takes your mind off the distance and physical aspects of your effort.

- Change your routine: Periodically find a more scenic route - such as a park or nature trail.

# My Walking Goal

I will:

| Date: | Time: | Location: | | Distance: |
|---|---|---|---|---|
| Weather: ☀ ☁ 🌧 | Type of Walk:  Light  Moderate  Strenuous | | | Companions: |

On a scale of 1 to 10, my walk today was:

Energetic                                              Exhausting
0 -- 1 -- 2 -- 3 -- 4 -- 5 -- 6 -- 7 -- 8 -- 9 -- 10

Today's sights, sounds, and smells:

_____
_____
_____
_____
_____
_____
_____
_____
_____
_____
_____
_____

Insights, thoughts and feelings:

| Date: | Time: | Location: | | Distance: |
|---|---|---|---|---|
| Weather: ☀ ☁ 🌧 | Type of Walk:    Light    Moderate    Strenuous | | Companions: | |

On a scale of 1 to 10, my walk today was:

    Energetic                        Exhausting
0 -- 1 -- 2 -- 3 -- 4 -- 5 -- 6 -- 7 -- 8 -- 9 -- 10

Today's sights, sounds, and smells:

___
___
___
___
___
___
___
___
___
___

> *Solvitur ambulando*, St. Jerome was fond of saying. To solve a problem, walk around.
>
> ~Gregory McNamee

Insights, thoughts and feelings:

| Date: | Time: | Location: | | Distance: |
|---|---|---|---|---|
| Weather: ☀ ☁ 🌧 | Type of Walk:    Light    Moderate    Strenuous | | Companions: | |

On a scale of 1 to 10, my walk today was:

> Energetic                                Exhausting
> 0 -- 1 -- 2 -- 3 -- 4 -- 5 -- 6 -- 7 -- 8 -- 9 -- 10

Today's sights, sounds, and smells:

_____
_____
_____
_____
_____
_____
_____
_____
_____
_____
_____

Insights, thoughts and feelings:

| Date: | Time: | Location: | Distance: |
|---|---|---|---|
| Weather: | Type of Walk:  Light   Moderate   Strenuous | | Companions: |

On a scale of 1 to 10, my walk today was:

Energetic                                          Exhausting
0 -- 1 -- 2 -- 3 -- 4 -- 5 -- 6 -- 7 -- 8 -- 9 -- 10

Today's sights, sounds, and smells:

_____
_____
_____
_____
_____
_____
_____
_____
_____
_____
_____

Insights, thoughts and feelings:

| Date: | Time: | Location: | | Distance: |
|---|---|---|---|---|
| Weather: ☼ ☁ ☂ | Type of Walk: <br><br> Light    Moderate    Strenuous | | Companions: | |

On a scale of 1 to 10, my walk today was:

Energetic                      Exhausting

0 -- 1 -- 2 -- 3 -- 4 -- 5 -- 6 -- 7 -- 8 -- 9 -- 10

Today's sights, sounds, and smells:

_____
_____
_____
_____
_____
_____
_____
_____
_____
_____
_____

> Walking takes longer... than any other known form of locomotion except crawling. Thus it stretches time and prolongs life. Life is already too short to waste on speed. ~ Edward Abbey, "Walking"

## Insights, thoughts and feelings:

| Date: | Time: | Location: | Distance: |
|---|---|---|---|
| | | | |

| Weather: | Type of Walk: | | | Companions: |
|---|---|---|---|---|
| ☀ ☁ ☂ | Light | Moderate | Strenuous | |

On a scale of 1 to 10, my walk today was:

Energetic                                                Exhausting
0 -- 1 -- 2 -- 3 -- 4 -- 5 -- 6 -- 7 -- 8 -- 9 -- 10

Today's sights, sounds, and smells:

_____
_____
_____
_____
_____
_____
_____
_____
_____
_____
_____

Insights, thoughts and feelings:

| Date: | Time: | Location: | | Distance: |
|---|---|---|---|---|
| Weather: ☀ ☁ 🌧 | Type of Walk: Light    Moderate    Strenuous | | Companions: | |

On a scale of 1 to 10, my walk today was:

Energetic                                    Exhausting
0 -- 1 -- 2 -- 3 -- 4 -- 5 -- 6 -- 7 -- 8 -- 9 -- 10

Today's sights, sounds, and smells:

_____
_____
_____
_____
_____
_____
_____
_____
_____
_____
_____

> A vigorous five-mile walk will do more good for an unhappy but otherwise healthy adult than all the medicine and psychology in the world.
>
> ~ Paul Dudley White

Insights, thoughts and feelings:

| Date: | Time: | Location: | | Distance: |
|---|---|---|---|---|
| Weather: ☀ ☁ ☂ | Type of Walk:  Light   Moderate   Strenuous | | Companions: | |

On a scale of 1 to 10, my walk today was:

```
       Energetic                        Exhausting
    0 -- 1 -- 2 -- 3 -- 4 -- 5 -- 6 -- 7 -- 8 -- 9 -- 10
```

Today's sights, sounds, and smells:

_____
_____
_____
_____
_____
_____
_____
_____
_____
_____
_____

Insights, thoughts and feelings:

| Date: | Time: | Location: | | Distance: |
|---|---|---|---|---|
| Weather: | Type of Walk: | | | Companions: |
| | Light | Moderate | Strenuous | |

On a scale of 1 to 10, my walk today was:

Energetic                                    Exhausting
0 -- 1 -- 2 -- 3 -- 4 -- 5 -- 6 -- 7 -- 8 -- 9 -- 10

Today's sights, sounds, and smells:

_____
_____
_____
_____
_____
_____
_____
_____
_____
_____
_____
_____

> I only went out for a walk and finally concluded to stay out till sundown, for going out, I found, was really going in.
> ~John Muir

Insights, thoughts and feelings:

| Date: | Time: | Location: | Distance: |
|---|---|---|---|
| | | | |

| Weather: ☀ ☁ ☂ | Type of Walk: Light  Moderate  Strenuous | Companions: |
|---|---|---|

On a scale of 1 to 10, my walk today was:

Energetic                                         Exhausting
0 -- 1 -- 2 -- 3 -- 4 -- 5 -- 6 -- 7 -- 8 -- 9 -- 10

Today's sights, sounds, and smells:

_____
_____
_____
_____
_____
_____
_____
_____
_____
_____
_____
_____

Insights, thoughts and feelings:

| Date: | Time: | Location: | | Distance: |
|---|---|---|---|---|
| Weather: | Type of Walk: | | | Companions: |
| | Light | Moderate | Strenuous | |

On a scale of 1 to 10, my walk today was:

Energetic                                           Exhausting
0 -- 1 -- 2 -- 3 -- 4 -- 5 -- 6 -- 7 -- 8 -- 9 -- 10

Today's sights, sounds, and smells:

_____

_____

_____

_____

_____

_____

_____

_____

_____

_____

> Thoughts come clearly while one walks.
> ~Thomas Mann

Insights, thoughts and feelings:

| Date: | Time: | Location: | Distance: |
|---|---|---|---|
| Weather: ☀ ☁ ☂ | Type of Walk:  Light   Moderate   Strenuous | | Companions: |

On a scale of 1 to 10, my walk today was:

```
     Energetic                          Exhausting
   0 -- 1 -- 2 -- 3 -- 4 -- 5 -- 6 -- 7 -- 8 -- 9 -- 10
```

Today's sights, sounds, and smells:

_____
_____
_____
_____
_____
_____
_____
_____
_____
_____
_____

Insights, thoughts and feelings:

| Date: | Time: | Location: | | Distance: |
|---|---|---|---|---|
| Weather: | Type of Walk: Light   Moderate   Strenuous | | | Companions: |

On a scale of 1 to 10, my walk today was:

Energetic                                    Exhausting
0 -- 1 -- 2 -- 3 -- 4 -- 5 -- 6 -- 7 -- 8 -- 9 -- 10

Today's sights, sounds, and smells:

_____
_____
_____
_____
_____
_____
_____
_____
_____
_____
_____
_____

> People say that losing weight is no walk in the park. When I hear that I think, yeah, that's the problem. ~Chris Adam

## Insights, thoughts and feelings:

| Date: | Time: | Location: | | Distance: |
|---|---|---|---|---|
| Weather: ☀ ☁ 🌧 | Type of Walk:  Light   Moderate   Strenuous | | Companions: | |

On a scale of 1 to 10, my walk today was:

> Energetic                                  Exhausting
> 0 -- 1 -- 2 -- 3 -- 4 -- 5 -- 6 -- 7 -- 8 -- 9 -- 10

Today's sights, sounds, and smells:

_____

_____

_____

_____

_____

_____

_____

_____

_____

_____

Insights, thoughts and feelings:

| Date: | Time: | Location: | | Distance: |
|---|---|---|---|---|
| Weather: | Type of Walk: | | | Companions: |
| | Light | Moderate | Strenuous | |

On a scale of 1 to 10, my walk today was:

Energetic                               Exhausting
0 -- 1 -- 2 -- 3 -- 4 -- 5 -- 6 -- 7 -- 8 -- 9 -- 10

Today's sights, sounds, and smells:

_____
_____
_____
_____
_____
_____
_____
_____
_____
_____
_____

> Make your feet your friend. ~ J.M. Barrie

Insights, thoughts and feelings:

| Date: | Time: | Location: | | Distance: |
|---|---|---|---|---|
| Weather: ☀ ☁ ☂ | Type of Walk:     Light     Moderate     Strenuous | | Companions: | |

On a scale of 1 to 10, my walk today was:

> Energetic                        Exhausting
> 0 -- 1 -- 2 -- 3 -- 4 -- 5 -- 6 -- 7 -- 8 -- 9 -- 10

Today's sights, sounds, and smells:

_____
_____
_____
_____
_____
_____
_____
_____
_____
_____

Insights, thoughts and feelings:

| Date: | Time: | Location: | Distance: |
|---|---|---|---|

| Weather: | Type of Walk: Light   Moderate   Strenuous | Companions: |
|---|---|---|

On a scale of 1 to 10, my walk today was:

Energetic                              Exhausting
0 -- 1 -- 2 -- 3 -- 4 -- 5 -- 6 -- 7 -- 8 -- 9 -- 10

Today's sights, sounds, and smells:

_____
_____
_____
_____
_____
_____
_____
_____
_____
_____

> The best remedy for a short temper is a long walk.
>
> ~ Jacqueline Schiff

Insights, thoughts and feelings:

| Date: | Time: | Location: | Distance: |
|---|---|---|---|
| Weather: | Type of Walk:    Light    Moderate    Strenuous | | Companions: |

On a scale of 1 to 10, my walk today was:

Energetic                            Exhausting
0 -- 1 -- 2 -- 3 -- 4 -- 5 -- 6 -- 7 -- 8 -- 9 -- 10

Today's sights, sounds, and smells:

_____
_____
_____
_____
_____
_____
_____
_____
_____
_____
_____

Insights, thoughts and feelings:

| Date: | Time: | Location: | Distance: |
|---|---|---|---|
| | | | |

| Weather: | Type of Walk: | | | Companions: |
|---|---|---|---|---|
| ☀ ☁ ☔ | Light | Moderate | Strenuous | |

On a scale of 1 to 10, my walk today was:

> Energetic                                            Exhausting
> 0 -- 1 -- 2 -- 3 -- 4 -- 5 -- 6 -- 7 -- 8 -- 9 -- 10

Today's sights, sounds, and smells:

_____
_____
_____
_____
_____
_____
_____
_____
_____
_____

> We live in a fast-paced society. Walking slows us down.
>
> ~ Robert Sweetgall

Insights, thoughts and feelings:

| Date: | Time: | Location: | | Distance: |
|---|---|---|---|---|

| Weather: | Type of Walk: | | | Companions: |
|---|---|---|---|---|
| ☀ ☁ ☂ | Light | Moderate | Strenuous | |

On a scale of 1 to 10, my walk today was:

Energetic                                         Exhausting
0 -- 1 -- 2 -- 3 -- 4 -- 5 -- 6 -- 7 -- 8 -- 9 -- 10

Today's sights, sounds, and smells:

_____
_____
_____
_____
_____
_____
_____
_____
_____
_____
_____
_____

Insights, thoughts and feelings:

| Date: | Time: | Location: | | Distance: |
|---|---|---|---|---|
| Weather: ☀ ☁ ☂ | Type of Walk:    Light   Moderate   Strenuous | | Companions: | |

On a scale of 1 to 10, my walk today was:

> Energetic                          Exhausting
> 0 -- 1 -- 2 -- 3 -- 4 -- 5 -- 6 -- 7 -- 8 -- 9 -- 10

Today's sights, sounds, and smells:

_____

_____

_____

_____

_____

_____

_____

_____

_____

_____

_____

> We ought to take outdoor walks, to refresh and raise our spirits by deep breathing in the open air.
>
> ~ Lucius Annaeus Seneca

Insights, thoughts and feelings:

| Date: | Time: | Location: | | Distance: |
|---|---|---|---|---|
| Weather: ☀ ☁ ☂ | Type of Walk:     Light     Moderate     Strenuous | | Companions: | |

On a scale of 1 to 10, my walk today was:

> Energetic                         Exhausting
> 0 -- 1 -- 2 -- 3 -- 4 -- 5 -- 6 -- 7 -- 8 -- 9 -- 10

Today's sights, sounds, and smells:

_____
_____
_____
_____
_____
_____
_____
_____
_____
_____
_____

Insights, thoughts and feelings:

| Date: | Time: | Location: | Distance: |
|---|---|---|---|
| | | | |

| Weather: | Type of Walk: | | | Companions: |
|---|---|---|---|---|
| ☀ ☁ ☂ | Light | Moderate | Strenuous | |

On a scale of 1 to 10, my walk today was:

Energetic                                    Exhausting
0 -- 1 -- 2 -- 3 -- 4 -- 5 -- 6 -- 7 -- 8 -- 9 -- 10

Today's sights, sounds, and smells:

_____
_____
_____
_____
_____
_____
_____
_____
_____
_____
_____
_____
_____

> It is not easy to walk alone in the country without musing upon something.
>
> ~Charles Dickens

Insights, thoughts and feelings:

| Date: | Time: | Location: | | Distance: |
|---|---|---|---|---|
| Weather: ☀ ☁ ☂ | Type of Walk: <br><br> Light    Moderate    Strenuous | | Companions: | |

On a scale of 1 to 10, my walk today was:

> Energetic                       Exhausting
> 0 -- 1 -- 2 -- 3 -- 4 -- 5 -- 6 -- 7 -- 8 -- 9 -- 10

Today's sights, sounds, and smells:

_____
_____
_____
_____
_____
_____
_____
_____
_____
_____
_____

Insights, thoughts and feelings:

| Date: | Time: | Location: | | Distance: |
|---|---|---|---|---|

| Weather: ☀ ☁ ☂ | Type of Walk:  Light   Moderate   Strenuous | Companions: |
|---|---|---|

On a scale of 1 to 10, my walk today was:

Energetic                                              Exhausting
0 -- 1 -- 2 -- 3 -- 4 -- 5 -- 6 -- 7 -- 8 -- 9 -- 10

Today's sights, sounds, and smells:

_____
_____
_____
_____
_____
_____
_____
_____
_____
_____
_____
_____

> Walking is good for solving problems, it's like the feet are little psychiatrists.
>
> ~ Terri Guillemets

Insights, thoughts and feelings:

| Date: | Time: | Location: | Distance: |
|---|---|---|---|

| Weather: | Type of Walk: Light   Moderate   Strenuous | Companions: |
|---|---|---|

On a scale of 1 to 10, my walk today was:

```
     Energetic                          Exhausting
  0 -- 1 -- 2 -- 3 -- 4 -- 5 -- 6 -- 7 -- 8 -- 9 -- 10
```

Today's sights, sounds, and smells:

Insights, thoughts and feelings:

| Date: | Time: | Location: | Distance: |
|---|---|---|---|
| | | | |

| Weather: | Type of Walk: | | | Companions: |
|---|---|---|---|---|
| | Light | Moderate | Strenuous | |

On a scale of 1 to 10, my walk today was:

Energetic                                    Exhausting
0 -- 1 -- 2 -- 3 -- 4 -- 5 -- 6 -- 7 -- 8 -- 9 -- 10

Today's sights, sounds, and smells:

_____
_____
_____
_____
_____
_____
_____
_____
_____
_____
_____
_____

> I stroll along serenely, with my eyes, my shoes my rage, forgetting everything.
> ~Pablo Neruda

Insights, thoughts and feelings:

| Date: | Time: | Location: | | Distance: |
|---|---|---|---|---|
| Weather: | Type of Walk: Light  Moderate  Strenuous | | | Companions: |

On a scale of 1 to 10, my walk today was:

Energetic                                      Exhausting
0 -- 1 -- 2 -- 3 -- 4 -- 5 -- 6 -- 7 -- 8 -- 9 -- 10

Today's sights, sounds, and smells:

_____
_____
_____
_____
_____
_____
_____
_____
_____
_____
_____

Insights, thoughts and feelings:

| Date: | Time: | Location: | Distance: |
|---|---|---|---|
| | | | |

| Weather: | Type of Walk: | | | Companions: |
|---|---|---|---|---|
| ☀ ☁ ☂ | Light | Moderate | Strenuous | |

On a scale of 1 to 10, my walk today was:

Energetic                                      Exhausting
0 -- 1 -- 2 -- 3 -- 4 -- 5 -- 6 -- 7 -- 8 -- 9 -- 10

Today's sights, sounds, and smells:

_____
_____
_____
_____
_____
_____
_____
_____
_____
_____
_____

> All truly great thoughts are conceived by walking.
>
> ~Friedrich Nietzsche

Insights, thoughts and feelings:

| Date: | Time: | Location: | Distance: |
|---|---|---|---|
| Weather: ☀ ☁ ☂ | Type of Walk:    Light    Moderate    Strenuous | | Companions: |

On a scale of 1 to 10, my walk today was:

> Energetic                                      Exhausting
> 0 -- 1 -- 2 -- 3 -- 4 -- 5 -- 6 -- 7 -- 8 -- 9 -- 10

Today's sights, sounds, and smells:

_____
_____
_____
_____
_____
_____
_____
_____
_____
_____
_____

Insights, thoughts and feelings:

| Date: | Time: | Location: | | Distance: |
|---|---|---|---|---|
| Weather: ☀ ☁ ☂ | Type of Walk:  Light   Moderate   Strenuous | | | Companions: |

On a scale of 1 to 10, my walk today was:

```
   Energetic                              Exhausting
  0 -- 1 -- 2 -- 3 -- 4 -- 5 -- 6 -- 7 -- 8 -- 9 -- 10
```

Today's sights, sounds, and smells:
_____
_____
_____
_____
_____
_____
_____
_____
_____
_____
_____
_____

> Of all exercises walking is the best.
>
> ~ Thomas Jefferson

Insights, thoughts and feelings:

| Date: | Time: | Location: | | Distance: |
|---|---|---|---|---|

| Weather: | Type of Walk: | | | Companions: |
|---|---|---|---|---|
| | Light | Moderate | Strenuous | |

On a scale of 1 to 10, my walk today was:

Energetic										Exhausting
0 -- 1 -- 2 -- 3 -- 4 -- 5 -- 6 -- 7 -- 8 -- 9 -- 10

Today's sights, sounds, and smells:

_____
_____
_____
_____
_____
_____
_____
_____
_____
_____

Insights, thoughts and feelings:

| Date: | Time: | Location: | | Distance: |
|---|---|---|---|---|

| Weather: | Type of Walk: | | | Companions: |
|---|---|---|---|---|
| | Light | Moderate | Strenuous | |

On a scale of 1 to 10, my walk today was:

> Energetic                                           Exhausting
> 0 -- 1 -- 2 -- 3 -- 4 -- 5 -- 6 -- 7 -- 8 -- 9 -- 10

Today's sights, sounds, and smells:

_____
_____
_____
_____
_____
_____
_____
_____
_____
_____

> In every walk with nature one receives
> far more than he seeks.
>
> ~ John Muir

## Insights, thoughts and feelings:

| Date: | Time: | Location: | Distance: |
|---|---|---|---|
| Weather: | Type of Walk:  Light   Moderate   Strenuous | | Companions: |

On a scale of 1 to 10, my walk today was:

Energetic                                    Exhausting
0 -- 1 -- 2 -- 3 -- 4 -- 5 -- 6 -- 7 -- 8 -- 9 -- 10

Today's sights, sounds, and smells:

_____
_____
_____
_____
_____
_____
_____
_____
_____
_____
_____
_____

Insights, thoughts and feelings:

| Date: | Time: | Location: | | Distance: |
|---|---|---|---|---|
| Weather: | Type of Walk: Light   Moderate   Strenuous | | | Companions: |

On a scale of 1 to 10, my walk today was:

Energetic                                    Exhausting
0 -- 1 -- 2 -- 3 -- 4 -- 5 -- 6 -- 7 -- 8 -- 9 -- 10

Today's sights, sounds, and smells:
_____
_____
_____
_____
_____
_____
_____
_____
_____
_____
_____

> "Above all, do not lose your desire to walk. Every day I walk myself into a state of well-being and walk away from every illness. I have walked myself into my best thoughts, and I know of no thought so burdensome that one cannot walk away from it." ~ Soren Kierkegaard

## Insights, thoughts and feelings:

| Date: | Time: | Location: | | Distance: |
|---|---|---|---|---|
| Weather: | Type of Walk:  Light   Moderate   Strenuous | | Companions: | |

On a scale of 1 to 10, my walk today was:

Energetic                                    Exhausting
0 -- 1 -- 2 -- 3 -- 4 -- 5 -- 6 -- 7 -- 8 -- 9 -- 10

Today's sights, sounds, and smells:

_____
_____
_____
_____
_____
_____
_____
_____
_____
_____
_____

Insights, thoughts and feelings:

| Date: | Time: | Location: | | Distance: |
|---|---|---|---|---|
| Weather: | Type of Walk:  Light    Moderate    Strenuous | | | Companions: |

On a scale of 1 to 10, my walk today was:

Energetic                                         Exhausting
0 -- 1 -- 2 -- 3 -- 4 -- 5 -- 6 -- 7 -- 8 -- 9 -- 10

Today's sights, sounds, and smells:

_____
_____
_____
_____
_____
_____
_____
_____
_____
_____

> *All walking is discovery. On foot we take the time to see things whole.*
>
> ~ Hal Borland

Insights, thoughts and feelings:

| Date: | Time: | Location: | | Distance: |
|---|---|---|---|---|
| Weather: | Type of Walk: | | | Companions: |
| | Light | Moderate | Strenuous | |

On a scale of 1 to 10, my walk today was:

Energetic                                                   Exhausting
0 -- 1 -- 2 -- 3 -- 4 -- 5 -- 6 -- 7 -- 8 -- 9 -- 10

Today's sights, sounds, and smells:

_____
_____
_____
_____
_____
_____
_____
_____
_____
_____

Insights, thoughts and feelings:

| Date: | Time: | Location: | | Distance: |
|---|---|---|---|---|
| Weather: ☀ ☁ ☂ | Type of Walk:  Light   Moderate   Strenuous | | Companions: | |

On a scale of 1 to 10, my walk today was:

```
   Energetic                              Exhausting
0 -- 1 -- 2 -- 3 -- 4 -- 5 -- 6 -- 7 -- 8 -- 9 -- 10
```

Today's sights, sounds, and smells:

_____
_____
_____
_____
_____
_____
_____
_____
_____
_____
_____
_____

> Walking is a man's best medicine.
>
> - Hippocrates

Insights, thoughts and feelings:

| Date: | Time: | Location: | | Distance: |
|---|---|---|---|---|
| Weather: ☀ ☁ ☂ | Type of Walk:  Light    Moderate    Strenuous | | Companions: | |

On a scale of 1 to 10, my walk today was:

Energetic                                  Exhausting
0 -- 1 -- 2 -- 3 -- 4 -- 5 -- 6 -- 7 -- 8 -- 9 -- 10

Today's sights, sounds, and smells:

___
___
___
___
___
___
___
___
___
___

Insights, thoughts and feelings:

| Date: | Time: | Location: | | Distance: |
|---|---|---|---|---|
| Weather: ☀ ☁ ☁ | Type of Walk: Light  Moderate  Strenuous | | | Companions: |

On a scale of 1 to 10, my walk today was:

Energetic                                      Exhausting
0 -- 1 -- 2 -- 3 -- 4 -- 5 -- 6 -- 7 -- 8 -- 9 -- 10

Today's sights, sounds, and smells:

___
___
___
___
___
___
___
___
___
___

> When you walk in the mountains stands of cedar, among the wise old elder trees, anything you want to know you can find there.
>
> – Saying of the Lummi Tribe of Puget Sound

Insights, thoughts and feelings:

| Date: | Time: | Location: | | Distance: |
|---|---|---|---|---|
| Weather: | Type of Walk:  Light    Moderate    Strenuous | | | Companions: |

On a scale of 1 to 10, my walk today was:

```
      Energetic                              Exhausting
   0 -- 1 -- 2 -- 3 -- 4 -- 5 -- 6 -- 7 -- 8 -- 9 -- 10
```

Today's sights, sounds, and smells:

_____
_____
_____
_____
_____
_____
_____
_____
_____
_____
_____
_____

Insights, thoughts and feelings:

| Date: | Time: | Location: | | Distance: |
|---|---|---|---|---|
| Weather: ☀ ☁ ☂ | Type of Walk:  Light   Moderate   Strenuous | | | Companions: |

On a scale of 1 to 10, my walk today was:

Energetic                              Exhausting
0 -- 1 -- 2 -- 3 -- 4 -- 5 -- 6 -- 7 -- 8 -- 9 -- 10

Today's sights, sounds, and smells:

_____
_____
_____
_____
_____
_____
_____
_____
_____
_____

> Walking would teach people the quality that youngsters find so hard to learn - patience.
>
> - Edward P. Weston

Insights, thoughts and feelings:

| Date: | Time: | Location: | Distance: |
|---|---|---|---|
| | | | |

| Weather: | Type of Walk: | Companions: |
|---|---|---|
| ☀ ☁ ☂ | Light    Moderate    Strenuous | |

On a scale of 1 to 10, my walk today was:

Energetic                                    Exhausting
0 -- 1 -- 2 -- 3 -- 4 -- 5 -- 6 -- 7 -- 8 -- 9 -- 10

Today's sights, sounds, and smells:

_____
_____
_____
_____
_____
_____
_____
_____
_____
_____
_____
_____

Insights, thoughts and feelings:

| Date: | Time: | Location: | | Distance: |
|---|---|---|---|---|
| Weather: | Type of Walk: | | | Companions: |
| | Light | Moderate | Strenuous | |

On a scale of 1 to 10, my walk today was:

Energetic                                   Exhausting
0 -- 1 -- 2 -- 3 -- 4 -- 5 -- 6 -- 7 -- 8 -- 9 -- 10

Today's sights, sounds, and smells:

_____
_____
_____
_____
_____
_____
_____
_____
_____
_____
_____
_____

> Hiking is the best workout! ... You can hike for three hours and not even realize you're working out. And, hiking alone lets me have some time to myself.
>
> – Jamie Luner

## Insights, thoughts and feelings:

| Date: | Time: | Location: | | Distance: |
|---|---|---|---|---|
| Weather: ☀ ☁ ☂ | Type of Walk:  Light   Moderate   Strenuous | | Companions: | |

On a scale of 1 to 10, my walk today was:

Energetic                                   Exhausting
0 -- 1 -- 2 -- 3 -- 4 -- 5 -- 6 -- 7 -- 8 -- 9 -- 10

Today's sights, sounds, and smells:

Insights, thoughts and feelings:

| Date: | Time: | Location: | | Distance: |
|---|---|---|---|---|
| Weather: ☀ ☁ 🌧 | Type of Walk: Light　Moderate　Strenuous | | Companions: | |

On a scale of 1 to 10, my walk today was:

```
     Energetic                              Exhausting
   0 -- 1 -- 2 -- 3 -- 4 -- 5 -- 6 -- 7 -- 8 -- 9 -- 10
```

Today's sights, sounds, and smells:

_____
_____
_____
_____
_____
_____
_____
_____
_____
_____
_____

> As you sit on the hillside, or lie prone under the trees of the forest, or sprawl wet-legged by a mountain stream, the great door, that does not look like a door, opens.
>
> – Stephen Graham

## Insights, thoughts and feelings:

| Date: | Time: | Location: | | Distance: |
|---|---|---|---|---|
| Weather: | Type of Walk: | | | Companions: |
| | Light | Moderate | Strenuous | |

On a scale of 1 to 10, my walk today was:

Energetic　　　　　　　　　　　　Exhausting
0 -- 1 -- 2 -- 3 -- 4 -- 5 -- 6 -- 7 -- 8 -- 9 -- 10

Today's sights, sounds, and smells:
_____
_____
_____
_____
_____
_____
_____
_____
_____
_____
_____

Insights, thoughts and feelings:

| Date: | Time: | Location: | | Distance: |
|---|---|---|---|---|
| Weather: ☀ ☁ 🌧 | Type of Walk:<br><br>Light  Moderate  Strenuous | | Companions: | |

On a scale of 1 to 10, my walk today was:

> Energetic                                         Exhausting
> 0 -- 1 -- 2 -- 3 -- 4 -- 5 -- 6 -- 7 -- 8 -- 9 -- 10

Today's sights, sounds, and smells:

_____
_____
_____
_____
_____
_____
_____
_____
_____
_____

> Few people know how to take a walk. The qualifications are endurance, plain clothes, old shoes, an eye for nature, good humor, vast curiosity, good speech, good silence and nothing too much. - Ralph Waldo Emerson

Insights, thoughts and feelings:

| Date: | Time: | Location: | | Distance: |
|---|---|---|---|---|
| Weather: | Type of Walk:  Light    Moderate    Strenuous | | Companions: | |

On a scale of 1 to 10, my walk today was:

Energetic                                       Exhausting
0 -- 1 -- 2 -- 3 -- 4 -- 5 -- 6 -- 7 -- 8 -- 9 -- 10

Today's sights, sounds, and smells:

Insights, thoughts and feelings:

| Date: | Time: | Location: | | Distance: |
|---|---|---|---|---|
| Weather: | Type of Walk:  Light   Moderate   Strenuous | | Companions: | |

On a scale of 1 to 10, my walk today was:

Energetic                                  Exhausting
0 -- 1 -- 2 -- 3 -- 4 -- 5 -- 6 -- 7 -- 8 -- 9 -- 10

Today's sights, sounds, and smells:

> *If you are walking to seek, ye shall find."*
>
> — Sommeil Liberosensa

Insights, thoughts and feelings:

| Date: | Time: | Location: | | Distance: |
|---|---|---|---|---|
| Weather: ☀ ☁ 🌧 | Type of Walk:  Light   Moderate   Strenuous | | | Companions: |

On a scale of 1 to 10, my walk today was:

Energetic                                      Exhausting
0 -- 1 -- 2 -- 3 -- 4 -- 5 -- 6 -- 7 -- 8 -- 9 -- 10

Today's sights, sounds, and smells:

Insights, thoughts and feelings:

| Date: | Time: | Location: | | Distance: |
|---|---|---|---|---|
| Weather: | Type of Walk: | | | Companions: |
| | Light | Moderate | Strenuous | |

On a scale of 1 to 10, my walk today was:

> Energetic                      Exhausting
> 0 -- 1 -- 2 -- 3 -- 4 -- 5 -- 6 -- 7 -- 8 -- 9 -- 10

Today's sights, sounds, and smells:

_____
_____
_____
_____
_____
_____
_____
_____
_____
_____
_____

> Slow down and enjoy life. It's not only the scenery you miss by going to fast - you also miss the sense of where you are going and why.
>
> - Eddie Cantor

Insights, thoughts and feelings:

| Date: | Time: | Location: | | Distance: |
|---|---|---|---|---|
| Weather: | Type of Walk: Light  Moderate  Strenuous | | Companions: | |

On a scale of 1 to 10, my walk today was:

```
  Energetic                        Exhausting
  0 -- 1 -- 2 -- 3 -- 4 -- 5 -- 6 -- 7 -- 8 -- 9 -- 10
```

Today's sights, sounds, and smells:

_____
_____
_____
_____
_____
_____
_____
_____
_____
_____
_____
_____

Insights, thoughts and feelings:

| Date: | Time: | Location: | Distance: |
|---|---|---|---|
| | | | |

| Weather: | Type of Walk: | | | Companions: |
|---|---|---|---|---|
| ☀ ☁ 🌧 | Light | Moderate | Strenuous | |

On a scale of 1 to 10, my walk today was:

> Energetic　　　　　　　　　　　　Exhausting
> 0 -- 1 -- 2 -- 3 -- 4 -- 5 -- 6 -- 7 -- 8 -- 9 -- 10

Today's sights, sounds, and smells:

_____
_____
_____
_____
_____
_____
_____
_____
_____
_____
_____

> Do not go where the path may lead, go instead where there is no path and leave a trail.
>
> - Ralph Waldo Emerson

## Insights, thoughts and feelings:

| Date: | Time: | Location: | | Distance: |
|---|---|---|---|---|
| Weather: ☀ ☁ ☂ | Type of Walk:     Light     Moderate     Strenuous | | | Companions: |

On a scale of 1 to 10, my walk today was:

> Energetic                               Exhausting
> 0 -- 1 -- 2 -- 3 -- 4 -- 5 -- 6 -- 7 -- 8 -- 9 -- 10

Today's sights, sounds, and smells:

_____
_____
_____
_____
_____
_____
_____
_____
_____
_____
_____

Insights, thoughts and feelings:

Visit us at:

www.wanderingwalksofwonder.com

Printed in Germany
by Amazon Distribution
GmbH, Leipzig